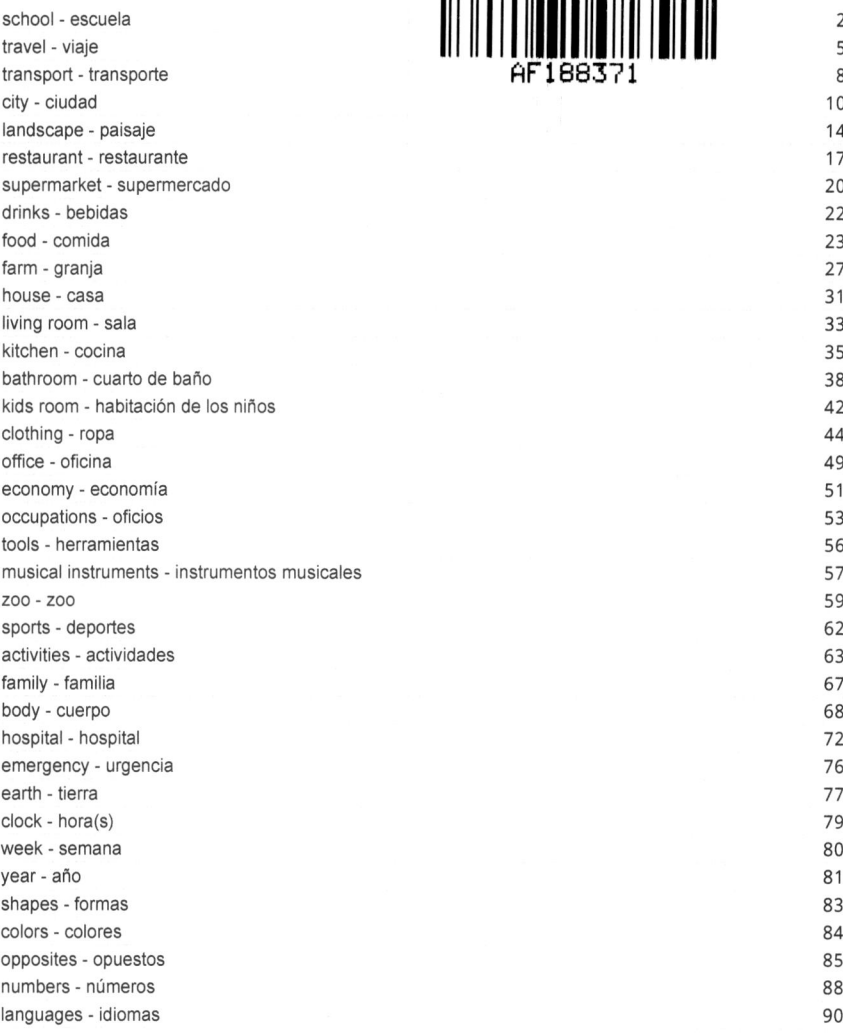

AF188371

Impressum
Verlag: BABADADA GmbH, Nedderfeld 112 , 22529 Hamburg
Geschäftsführer / Verlagsleitung: Harald Hof
Druck: Books on Demand GmbH, In de Tarpen 42, 22848 Norderstedt

Imprint
Publisher: BABADADA GmbH, Nedderfeld 112 , 22529 Hamburg, Germany
Managing Director / Publishing direction: Harald Hof
Print: Books on Demand GmbH, In de Tarpen 42, 22848 Norderstedt

classroom
aula

divide
dividir

186/2

school yard
patio

board
pizarra

teacher
maestro/a

paper
papel

write
escribir

pen
bolígrafo

desk
escritorio

ruler
regla

book
libro

pupil
alumno/a

satchel

cartera

pencil case

caja de lápices

pencil

lápiz

pencil sharpener

sacapuntas

rubber

goma de borrar

drawing pad

cuaderno de dibujo

drawing

dibujo

paintbrush

pincel

paint box

caja de pinturas

scissors

tijeras

glue

pegamento

exercise book

cuaderno de ejercicios

homework

deberes

number

número

add

sumar

subtract

restar

multiply

multiplicar

calculate

calcular

letter

letra

alphabet

alfabeto

word

palabra

text

texto

read

leer

chalk

tiza

lesson

lección

register

cuaderno de notas

examination

examen

certificate

certificado

school uniform

uniforme escolar

education

educación

encyclopedia

enciclopedia

university

universidad

microscope

microscopio

map

mapa

waste-paper basket

papelera

hotel
hotel

Grand

hostel
albergue

ROOMS

urrency exchange office
ficina de cambio de divisas

EXCHANGE

car
coche

language

idioma

yes / no

sí / no

Okay

Vale

hello

hola

translator

traductor

Thank you

Gracias

how much is...?

¿cuánto es...?

I don´t get it

No entiendo

problem

problema

Good evening!

¡Buenas tardes!

Good morning!

¡Buenos días!

Good night!

¡Buenas noches!

goodbye

adiós

direction

dirección

luggage

equipaje

bag

bolsa

backpack

mochila

guest

invitado

room

habitación

sleeping bag

saco de dormir

tent

tienda de campaña

tourist information

información turística

beach

playa

credit card

tarjeta de crédito

breakfast

desayuno

lunch

almuerzo

dinner

cena

Ticket

billete

elevator

ascensor

stamp

sello

border

frontera

customs

aduana

embassy

embajada

visa

visa

passport

pasaporte

airplane
avión

ship
barco

fire truck
coche de bomberos

truck
camión

bus
autobús

motorboat
lancha a motor

bike
bicicleta

car
coche

ferry

transbordador

boat

barca

motorbike

moto

police car

coche de policía

racing car

coche de carreras

rental car

coche de alquiler

car sharing	tow truck	garbage truck
préstamo de vehículos	grúa	camión de la basura
engine	fuel	fuel station
motor	gasolina	gasolinera
traffic sign	traffic	traffic jam
señal de tráfico	tráfico	atasco
parking lot	train station	tracks
aparcamiento	estación de tren	vías
train	tram	wagon
tren	tranvía	vagón

helicopter

helicóptero

airport

aeropuerto

tower

torre

passenger

pasajero

container

contenedor

carton

caja de cartón

cart

carretilla

basket

cesta

take off / land

despegar / aterrizar

city

ciudad

village

pueblo

city center

centro de ciudad

house

casa

movie theater
cine

advert
anuncio

street light
farola

CINEMA

street
calle

taxi
taxi

snack shop
quiosco

pedestrian
peatón

sidewalk
acera

zebra crossing
paso de cebra

umpster
ontenedor de basura

crossing
cruce

traffic lights
semáforo

hut
cabaña

apartment
apartamento

train station
estación de tren

city hall
ayuntamiento

museum
museo

school
escuela

university

universidad

bank

banco

hospital

hospital

hotel

hotel

pharmacy

farmacia

office

oficina

book shop

librería

shop

tienda

flower shop

floristería

supermarket

supermercado

market

mercado

department store

grandes almacenes

fishmonger's shop

pescadería

mall

centro comercial

harbor

puerto

city - ciudad

park

parque

bench

banco

bridge

puente

stairs

escaleras

subway

metro

tunnel

túnel

bus stop

parada de autobús

bar

bar

restaurant

restaurante

postbox

buzón

street sign

poste indicador

parking meter

parquímetro

zoo

zoo

swimming pool

piscina

mosque

mezquita

farm
granja

pollution
contaminación

cemetery
cementerio

church
iglesia

playground
patio de juego

temple
templo

landscape
paisaje

signpost
señal

path
camino

meadow
prado

stone
piedra

tree
árbol

hiker
excursionista

river
río

grass
hierba

flower
flor

valley

valle

hill

colina

lake

lago

forest

bosque

desert

desierto

volcano

volcán

castle

castillo

rainbow

arcoíris

mushroom

champiñón

palm tree

palmera

mosquito

mosquito

fly

mosca

ant

hormiga

bee

abeja

spider

araña

beetle

escarabajo

frog

rana

squirrel

ardilla

hedgehog

erizo

hare

liebre

owl

lechuza

bird

pájaro

swan

cisne

boar

jabalí

deer

ciervo

moose

alce

dam

presa

wind turbine

turbina eólica

solar panel

panel solar

climate

clima

landscape - paisaje

waiter
camarero

menu
menú

chair
silla

soup
sopa

pizza
pizza

cutlery
cubertería

tablecloth
mantel

starter
primer plato

main course
plato principal

dessert
postre

drinks
bebidas

food
comida

bottle
botella

fast food

comida rápida

street food

comida callejera

teapot

tetera

sugar bowl

azucarero

portion

porción

espresso machine

cafetera expreso

high chair

trona

bill

cuenta

tray

bandeja

knife

cuchillo

fork

tenedor

spoon

cuchara

teaspoon

cucharilla

serviette

servilleta

glass

vaso

plate
plato

soup plate
plato hondo

saucer
platillo

sauce
salsa

salt shaker
salero

pepper mill
molinillo de pimienta

vinegar
vinagre

oil
aceite

spices
especias

ketchup
ketchup

mustard
mostaza

mayonnaise
mayonesa

special offer
oferta especial

customer
cliente

dairy products
lácteos

FOR

fruit
fruta

shopping cart
carro de la compra

butcher's shop

carnicería

bakery

panadería

weigh

pesar

vegetables

verduras

meat

carne

frozen food

alimentos congelados

cold cuts

fiambres

canned food

conservas

detergent

detergente en polvo

candy

dulces

household products

productos de uso doméstico

cleaning products

productos de limpieza

sales representative

vendedora

cash register

caja

cashier

cajero

shopping list

lista de la compra

opening hours

horario de atención al público

wallet

cartera

credit card

tarjeta de crédito

bag

bolsa

plastic bag

bolsa de plástico

water

agua

juice

zumo

milk

leche

coke

cola

wine

vino

beer

cerveza

alcohol

alcohol

cocoa

cacao

tea

té

coffee

café

espresso

expreso

cappuccino

capuchino

banana

plátano

apple

manzana

orange

naranja

melon

melón

lemon

limón

carrot

zanahoria

garlic

ajo

bamboo

bambú

onion

cebolla

mushroom

champiñón

nuts

avellanas

noodles

fideos

spaghetti

espagueti

rice

arroz

salad

ensalada

fries

patatas fritas

fried potatoes

patatas fritas

pizza

pizza

hamburger

hamburguesa

sandwich

sándwich

escalope

filete

ham

jamón

salami

salami

sausage

salchicha

chicken

pollo

roast

asado

fish

pescado

porridge oats

copos de avena

muesli

muesli

cornflakes

copos de maíz

flour

harina

croissant

cruasán

bread roll

panecillo

bread

pan

toast

tostada

cookies

galletas

butter

mantequilla

curd

cuajada

cake

pastel

egg

huevo

fried egg

huevo frito

cheese

queso

ice cream	sugar	honey
helado	azúcar	miel

jelly	nougat cream	curry
mermelada	crema de turrón	curry

goat

cabra

cow

vaca

calf

ternero

pig

cerdo

piglet

cerdito

bull

toro

goose

ganso

duck

pato

chick

pollo

hen

gallina

cockerel

gallo

rat

rata

cat

gato

mouse

ratón

ox

buey

dog

perro

dog house

perrera

garden hose

manguera

watering can

regadera

scythe

guadaña

plow

arado

sickle

hoz

hoe

azada

pitchfork

horca

axe

hacha

pushcart

carretilla

trough

abrevadero

milk can

lechera

sack

saco

fence

valla

stable

establo

greenhouse

invernadero

soil

suelo

seed

semilla

fertilizer

fertilizador

combine harvester

cosechadora

harvest

cosechar

harvest

cosecha

yams

ñame

wheat

trigo

soya

soja

potato

patata

corn

maíz

rapeseed

semilla de colza

fruit tree

árbol frutal

manioc

mandioca

grain

cereales

living room
sala

bathroom
cuarto de baño

kitchen
cocina

bedroom
dormitorio

kids room
habitación de los niños

dining room
comedor

floor

suelo

wall

pared

ceiling

techo

cellar

sótano

sauna

sauna

balcony

balcón

terrace

terraza

pool

piscina

lawn mower

cortacésped

sheet

sábana

bedspread

colcha

bed

cama

broom

escoba

bucket

balde

switch

interruptor

carpet	drape	table
alfombra	cortina	mesa

chair	rocking chair	armchair
silla	mecedora	butaca

book

libro

blanket

manta

decoration

decoración

firewood

leña

film

película

stereo system

equipo de música

key

llave

newspaper

periódico

painting

pintura

poster

póster

radio

radio

notebook

cuaderno

vacuum cleaner

aspiradora

cactus

cactus

candle

vela

fridge
refrigerador

microwave oven
microondas

kitchen scales
balanza de cocina

toaster
tostadora

laundry detergent
detergente

stove
horno

freezer
congelador

dishwasher
lavavajillas

cooker
....
olla a presión

pot
....
olla

cast-iron pot
....
olla de hierro fundido

wok / kadai
....
wok / karahi

pan
....
cazuela

kettle
....
hervidor

steamer

vaporera

baking tray

chapa de horno

crockery

vajilla

mug

taza

bowl

tazón

chopsticks

palillos

ladle

cucharón

spatula

espumadera

whisk

batidor

strainer

colador

sieve

cedazo

grater

rallador

mortar

mortero

barbecue

barbacoa

fireplace

hoguera

chopping board

tabla de picar

rolling pin

rodillo

corkscrew

sacacorchos

can

lata

can opener

abrelatas

oven cloth

agarrador

sink

lavabo

brush

cepillo

sponge

esponja

blender

batidora

deep freezer

congelador

baby bottle

biberón

tap

grifo

cuarto de baño

heating
calefacción

shower
ducha

towel
toalla

shower curtain
cortina de la ducha

bubble bath
baño de espuma

bathtub
bañera

glass
vaso

washing machine
lavadora

tap
grifo

tiles
baldosas

potty
orinal

sink
lavabo

toilet
inodoro

squat toilet
inodoro rústico

bidet
bidé

urinal
urinario

toilet paper
papel higiénico

toilet brush
escobilla del váter

toothbrush

cepillo de dientes

toothpaste

pasta de dientes

dental floss

hilo dental

wash

lavar

hand shower

ducha de mano

douche

ducha íntima

basin

pila

back brush

cepillo de espalda

soap

jabón

shower gel

gel de ducha

shampoo

champú

flannel

toallita

drain

desagüe

creme

crema

deodorant

desodorante

mirror

espejo

hand mirror

espejo de tocador

razor

maquinilla de afeitar

shaving foam

espuma de afeitar

aftershave

loción postafeitado

comb

peine

brush

cepillo

hair-dryer

secador

hairspray

laca

makeup

maquillaje

lipstick

pintalabios

nail varnish

pintauñas

cotton wool

algodón

nail scissors

cortauñas

perfume

perfume

washbag

estuche de viaje

stool

banqueta

weighing scales

balanza

bathrobe

albornoz

rubber gloves

guantes de goma

tampon

tampón

sanitary towel

compresa

chemical toilet

inodoro químico

kids room
habitación de los niños

alarm clock
despertador

cuddly toy
peluche

toy car
coche de juguete

rattle
sonajero

doll's house
casa de muñecas

present
regalo

balloon
globo

bed
cama

stroller
coche de niño

deck of cards
naipes

jigsaw
puzle

comic
tebeo

lego bricks

piezas de lego

toy blocks

bloques de juguete

action figure

figura de acción

romper suit

bodi (de bebé)

frisbee

frisbee

mobile

colgador móvil para bebés

board game

juego de mesa

dice

dados

model train set

circuito de tren eléctrico

pacifier

maniquí

party

fiesta

picture book

álbum de fotos

ball

pelota

doll

muñeca

play

jugar

sandpit

cajón de arena

swing

columpio

toys

juguetes

video game console

videoconsola

tricycle

triciclo

teddy bear

oso de peluche

wardrobe

guardarropa

clothing

ropa

socks

calcetines

stockings

medias

tights

leotardos

scarf
bufanda

belt
cinturón

umbrella
paraguas

t-shirt
camiseta

boots
botas

slippers
zapatillas

sneakers
deportivas

sandals	shoes	rubber boots
sandalias	zapatos	botas de goma

underwear	bra	undershirt
slip	sostén	chaleco

body

bodi

pants

pantalones

jeans

vaqueros

skirt

falda

blouse

blusa

shirt

camisa

pullover

jersey

sweater

suéter

blazer

blazer

jacket

chaqueta

coat

abrigo

raincoat

gabardina

costume

traje

dress

vestido

wedding dress

vestido de novia

suit
traje

nightgown
camisón

pajamas
pijama

sari
sari

headscarf
bandana

turban
turbante

burka
burka

kaftan
caftán

abaya
abaya

swimsuit
traje de baño

trunks
bañador

shorts
pantalones cortos

tracksuit
chándal

apron
delantal

gloves
guantes

button

botón

glasses

gafas

bracelet

brazalete

necklace

collar

ring

anillo

earring

pendiente

cap

gorra

coat hanger

percha

hat

sombrero

tie

corbata

zip

cremallera

helmet

casco

braces

tirantes

school uniform

uniforme escolar

uniform

uniforme

bib
....
babero

pacifier
....
maniquí

diaper
....
pañal

office
oficina

server
servidor

filing cabinet
archivo

printer
impresora

paper
papel

monitor
monitor

mouse
ratón

desk
escritorio

folder
carpeta

keyboard
teclado

chair
silla

waste-paper basket
papelera

computer
ordenador

coffee mug
....
taza de café

calculator
....
calculadora

internet
....
internet

laptop

portátil

letter

carta

message

mensaje

cell phone

móvil

network

red

photocopier

fotocopiadora

software

software

telephone

teléfono

plug socket

toma de corriente

fax machine

fax

form

formulario

document

documento

office - oficina

buy

comprar

pay

pagar

trade

comerciar

money

dinero

dollar

dólar

euro

euro

yen

yen

rouble

rublo

Swiss franc

franco suizo

renminbi yuan

renminbi yuan

rupee

rupia

cash point

cajero automático

currency exchange office

oficina de cambio de divisas

gold

oro

silver

plata

oil

petróleo

energy

energía

price

precio

contract

contrato

tax

impuesto

stock

acción

work

trabajar

employee

empleado

employer

empleador

factory

fábrica

shop

tienda

economy - economía

police officer
agente de policía

fireman
bombero

cook
cocinero

doctor
médico

pilot
piloto

gardener

jardinero

carpenter

carpintero

seamstress

costurera

judge

juez

chemist

farmacéutico

actor

actor

bus driver

conductor de autobús

taxi driver

taxista

fisherman

pescador

cleaning lady

señora de la limpieza

roofer

techador

waiter

camarero

hunter

cazador

painter

pintor

baker

panadero

electrician

electricista

builder

obrero

engineer

ingeniero

butcher

carnicero

plumber

fontanero

postman

cartero

soldier

soldado

architect

arquitecto

cashier

cajero

florist

florista

hairdresser

peluquero

conductor

revisor

mechanic

mecánico

captain

capitán

dentist

dentista

scientist

científico

rabbi

rabino

imam

imán

monk

monje

pastor

sacerdote

hammer
martillo

pliers
alicates

screwdriver
destornillador

wrench
llave

torch
linterna

excavator

excavadora

toolbox

caja de herramientas

ladder

escalera de mano

saw

sierra

nails

clavos

drill

taladro

repair
reparar

shovel
pala

Damn!
¡Maldita sea!

dustpan
recogedor

paint can
bote de pintura

screws
tornillos

musical instruments
instrumentos musicales

loud speaker
altavoz

drum set
batería

guitar
guitarra

double bass
contrabajo

trumpet
trompeta

piano

piano

violin

violín

bass

bajo

timpani

timbales

drums

tambor

keyboard

teclado

saxophone

saxofón

flute

flauta

microphone

micrófono

musical instruments - instrumentos musicales

entrance
entrada

tiger
tigre

cage
jaula

zebra
cebra

animal feed
pienso

panda
panda

animals
animales

elephant
elefante

kangaroo
canguro

rhino
rinoceronte

gorilla
gorila

bear
oso

camel

camello

ostrich

avestruz

lion

león

monkey

mono

flamingo

flamingo

parrot

loro

polar bear

oso polar

penguin

pingüino

shark

tiburón

peacock

pavo real

snake

serpiente

crocodile

cocodrilo

zookeeper

guardián de zoológico

seal

foca

jaguar

jaguar

zoo - zoo

pony
poni

leopard
leopardo

hippo
hipopótamo

giraffe
jirafa

eagle
águila

boar
jabalí

fish
pescado

turtle
tortuga

walrus
morsa

fox
zorro

gazelle
gacela

American football
fútbol americano

cycling
ciclismo

tennis
tenis

basketball
baloncesto

swimming
natación

boxing
boxeo

ice hockey
hockey sobre hielo

soccer
fútbol

badminton
bádminton

athletics
atletismo

handball
balonmano

skiing
esquí

polo
polo

jump
saltar

laugh
reír

hug
abrazar

walk
caminar

sing
cantar

dream
soñar

pray
rezar

kiss
besar

write

escribir

draw

dibujar

show

mostrar

push

empujar

give

dar

take

tomar

have
....
tener

do
....
hacer

be
....
ser

stand
....
estar de pie

run
....
correr

pull
....
tirar

throw
....
tirar

fall
....
caer

lie
....
yacer

wait
....
esperar

carry
....
llevar

sit
....
estar sentado

get dressed
....
vestirse

sleep
....
dormir

wake up
....
despertar

activities - actividades

look at

mirar

cry

llorar

stroke

acariciar

comb

peinar

talk

hablar

understand

entender

ask

preguntar

listen

escuchar

drink

beber

eat

comer

tidy up

ordenar

love

amar

cook

cocinar

drive

conducir

fly

volar

activities - actividades

sail

navegar

calculate

calcular

read

leer

learn

aprender

work

trabajar

marry

casarse

sew

coser

brush teeth

cepillarse los dientes

kill

matar

smoke

fumar

send

enviar

grandmother
abuela

grandfather
abuelo

father
padre

mother
madre

baby
bebé

daughter
hija

son
hijo

guest

invitado

aunt

tía

uncle

tío

brother

hermano

sister

hermana

forehead
frente

eye
ojo

shoulder
hombro

finger
dedo

face
cara

chin
barbilla

hand
mano

breast
pecho

leg
pierna

arm
brazo

baby

bebé

man

hombre

woman

mujer

girl

chica

boy

chico

head

cabeza

back

espalda

belly

vientre

navel

ombligo

toe

dedo del pie

heel

talón

bone

hueso

hip

cadera

knee

rodilla

elbow

codo

nose

nariz

buttocks

trasero

skin

piel

cheek

mejilla

ear

oído

lip

labio

mouth

boca

tooth

diente

tongue

lengua

brain

cerebro

heart

corazón

muscle

músculo

lung

pulmón

liver

hígado

stomach

estómago

kidneys

riñones

sex

sexo

condom

condón

ovum

ovario

semen

semen

pregnancy

embarazo

body - cuerpo

menstruation
menstruación

vagina
vagina

penis
pene

eyebrow
ceja

hair
pelo

neck
cuello

hospital
hospital

ambulance
ambulancia

wheelchair
silla de ruedas

fracture
fractura

doctor

médico

emergency room

sala de urgencias

nurse

enfermera

emergency

urgencia

unconscious

inconsciente

pain

dolor

injury

lesión

bleeding

hemorragia

heart attack

infarto

stroke

ictus

allergy

alergia

cough

tos

fever

fiebre

flu

gripe

diarrhea

diarrea

headache

dolor de cabeza

cancer

cáncer

diabetes

diabetes

surgeon

cirujano

scalpel

bisturí

operation

operación

CT

TAC

x-ray

rayos x

ultrasound

ultrasonido

face mask

mascarilla

disease

enfermedad

waiting room

sala de espera

crutch

muleta

plaster

tirita

bandage

venda

injection

inyección

stethoscope

estetoscopio

stretcher

camilla

clinical thermometer

termómetro

birth

nacimiento

overweight

sobrepeso

hospital - hospital

hearing aid

audífono

disinfectant

desinfectante

infection

infección

virus

virus

HIV / AIDS

VIH / SIDA

medicine

medicina

vaccination

vacunación

tablets

tabletas

pill

pastilla

emergency call

llamada de urgencia

blood pressure monitor

tensiómetro

ill / healthy

enfermo / sano

Help!

¡Socorro!

alarm

alarma

assault

asalto

attack

ataque

danger

peligro

emergency exit

salida de emergencia

Fire!

¡Fuego!

fire extinguisher

extintor de incendios

accident

accidente

first-aid kit

botiquín de primeros
auxilios

SOS

SOS

police

policía

Europe

Europa

North America

Norteamérica

South America

Sudamérica

Africa

África

Asia

Asia

Australia

Australia

Atlantic

Atlántico

Pacific

Pacífico

Indian Ocean

Océano Índico

Antarctic Ocean

Océano Antártico

Arctic Ocean

Océano Ártico

North pole

polo norte

South pole
....
polo sur

Antarctica
....
Antártida

earth
....
tierra

land
....
tierra

sea
....
mar

island
....
isla

nation
....
nación

state
....
estado

clock face

esfera

hour hand

manecilla de las horas

minute hand

minutero

second hand

segundero

What time is it?

¿Qué hora es?

day

día

time

tiempo

now

ahora

digital watch

reloj digital

minute

minuto

hour

hora

week

semana

Monday
lunes

Wednesday
miércoles

Friday
viernes

Tuesday
martes

Saturday
sábado

Thursday
jueves

Sunday
domingo

yesterday

ayer

today

hoy

tomorrow

mañana

morning

mañana

noon

mediodía

evening

tarde

workdays

días laborables

weekend

fin de semana

rain
lluvia

snow
nieve

wind
viento

spring
primavera

fall
otoño

summer
verano

winter
invierno

weather forecast
....
pronóstico del tiempo

thermometer
....
termómetro

sunshine
....
sol

cloud
....
nube

fog
....
niebla

humidity
....
humedad

lightning

rayo

thunder

trueno

storm

tormenta

hail

granizo

monsoon

monzón

flood

inundación

ice

hielo

January

enero

February

febrero

March

marzo

April

abril

May

mayo

June

junio

July

julio

August

agosto

September
....
septiembre

October
....
octubre

November
....
noviembre

December
....
diciembre

shapes
formas

circle
....
círculo

square
....
cuadrado

rectangle
....
rectángulo

triangle
....
triángulo

sphere
....
esfera

cube
....
cubo

white
blanco

yellow
amarillo

orange
anaranjado

pink
rosa

red
rojo

purple
morado

blue
azul

green
verde

brown
marrón

gray
gris

black
negro

opposites
opuestos

a lot / a little

mucho / poco

angry / calm

enojado / tranquilo

beautiful / ugly

bonito / feo

beginning / end

principio / fin

big / small

grande / pequeño

bright / dark

claro / oscuro

brother / sister

hermano / hermana

clean / dirty

limpio / sucio

complete / incomplete

completo / incompleto

day / night

día / noche

dead / alive

muerto / vivo

wide / narrow

ancho / estrecho

edible / inedible

comestible / no comestible

evil / kind

malo / amable

excited / bored

entusiasmado / aburrido

fat / thin

gordo / delgado

first / last

primero / último

friend / enemy

amigo / enemigo

full / empty

lleno / vacío

hard / soft

duro / blando

heavy / light

pesado / ligero

hunger / thirst

hambre / sed

ill / healthy

enfermo / sano

illegal / legal

ilegal / legal

intelligent / stupid

inteligente / tonto

left / right

izquierda / derecha

near / far

cerca / lejos

opposites - opuestos

new / used

nuevo / usado

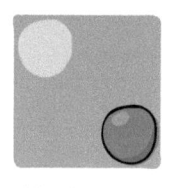

nothing / something

nada / algo

old / young

viejo / joven

on / off

encendido / apagado

open / closed

abierto / cerrado

quiet / loud

silencioso / ruidoso

rich / poor

rico / pobre

right / wrong

correcto / incorrecto

rough / smooth

áspero / suave

sad / happy

triste / contento

short / long

corto / largo

slow / fast

lento / rápido

wet / dry

húmedo / seco

warm / cool

cálido / frío

war / peace

guerra / paz

opposites - opuestos

0

zero

cero

1

one

uno

2

two

dos

3

three

tres

4

four

cuatro

5

five

cinco

6

six

seis

7

seven

siete

8

eight

ocho

9

nine

nueve

10

ten

diez

11

eleven

once

12

twelve

doce

13

thirteen

trece

14

fourteen

catorce

15

fifteen

quince

16

sixteen

dieciséis

17

seventeen

diecisiete

18

eighteen

dieciocho

19

nineteen

diecinueve

20

twenty

veinte

100

hundred

cien

1.000

thousand

mil

1.000.000

million

millón

numbers - números

English

inglés

American English

inglés americano

Chinese Mandarin

chino mandarín

Hindi

hindi

Spanish

español

French

francés

Arabic

árabe

Russian

ruso

Portuguese

portugués

Bengali

bengalí

German

alemán

Japanese

japonés

I
yo

you
tú

he / she / it
él / ella / ello

we
nosotros/as

you
vosotros/as

they
ellos/as

who?
¿quién?

what?
¿qué?

how?
¿cómo?

where?
¿dónde?

when?
¿cuándo?

name
nombre

behind

detrás

in

en

in front of

delante de

over

por encima de

on

sobre

under

debajo de

beside

junto a

between

entre

place

lugar